Old Fallowfield

Paul Chrystal

The Nico Ditch Earthwork is a six-mile long linear earthwork running between Ashton-under-Lyne and Stretford, probably dug as a defensive fortification between the 5th and 11th centuries from when the Romans left and the Normans arrived; it is for the most part 4–5 yards wide and up to 5 feet deep and runs through Platt Fields Park behind the boundary wall of Manchester High School for Girls where it is designated a Scheduled Ancient Monument. The ditch leaves Platt Fields at Platt Chapel and corresponds today with the modern administrative boundaries between Manchester and Stockport as well as between Manchester and Tameside. The earliest reference comes in a 1190-1212 charter detailing the granting of land in Audenshaw to the monks of the Kersal Cell in Salford; here the ditch is referred to as "Mykelldiche", and a *magnum fossatum*, "large ditch". The picture shows the ditch where it forms the boundary of Manchester High School for Girls and the Ashfield part of Platt Fields Park.

Text © Paul Chrystal, 2020.
First published in the United Kingdom, 2020,
by Stenlake Publishing Ltd.,
54-58 Mill Square,
Catrine, Ayrshire,
KA5 6RD

Telephone: 01290 551122
www.stenlake.co.uk

Printed by Blissetts,
Roslin Road,
Acton,
W3 8DH

ISBN 9781840338805

**The publishers regret that they cannot supply
copies of any pictures featured in this book.**

To Jonathan

Acknowledgements

My thanks to the following for permission to use images from their archives; their generosity has made this an immeasurably better book: Rachel Kneale, Archivist, Manchester Grammar School; Gwen Hobson and Pam Roberts, School Archivists, Manchester High School for Girls. Thanks also to Pat Harris, author of *Against the Odds: The Story of the FCJ Convent School, 1852-1985* who kindly allowed me to use images from her book.

Also available from Stenlake Publishing:
Old Didsbury (ISBN 9781840338676)

Introduction

Mention Fallowfield today and most people see droves of students plying back and forth to the city's universities, many from the University of Manchester's Fallowfield Campus – the Owens Park halls of residence, the Firs Botanical Grounds and Platt Fields Park, crowding the local bars and filling local restaurants and cafes – all very wonderful for the local economy and the ambience of the place. Indeed, these students help to make Fallowfield what it is today – a lively, leafy suburb benefitting from many cultures, diversity and entertainment.

Fallowfield has a rich and fertile history taking in the 8th century Nico Ditch earthwork; the Platts of Platt Hall and Platt's Field Park; and two of the country's leading independent schools – Manchester High School for Girls and Manchester Grammar School; Patricia Frederika Phoenix (née Manfield) better known as Coronation Street's Elsie Tanner, – one of our first 'sex symbols' – was born at St. Mary's Hospital in Fallowfield in 1923 while the 1893 FA Cup Final kicked off here behind Owens Park (Wolves beat Everton 1-0); in 1986 the UK's first drive-through McDonald's opened in Fallowfield.

Judith Rosemary Locke Chalmers OBE (born 1935) is best known for presenting the travel programme 'Wish You Were Here…?' from 1974 to 2003; in the 1960s, she presented 'Family Favourites' and 'Woman's Hour' on the radio and 'Come dancing' on TV. She also appeared as the original Susan in 'The Clitheroe Kid', and worked with Ken Dodd on his radio show. Born in Stockport, she was educated at Withington Girls' School, an independent day school in Wellington Road, Fallowfield.

In 2011 Fallowfield had a population of 15,211. In former times it was in Lancashire; it is three miles south of Manchester city centre and is bisected east-west by Wilmslow Road and north-south by Moseley Road and Wilbraham Road. Written records begin in 1317 with a deed referring to "Fallafeld". During the 14th century at least part of Fallowfield was held by Jordan de Fallafeld. In 1530 it was mentioned as "Falowfelde". The Platt Estate to the north was owned by the Platts and then by the Worsleys. In 1869 Wilbraham Road was built to connect Fallowfield with Edge Lane in Chorlton-cum-Hardy which spawned major development west of the Wilmslow Road. Mansions went up for, for example, Joseph Whitworth, "The Firs", and the Behrens family, "The Oaks". as well as the interestingly named Cabbage Hall.

The people who lived in this rural community did their well-dressing and performed the rushcart ceremony; they holidayed through the week-long Fallowfield Wakes which included clog shod rush dancing. The railways transformed life here from 1891 when Fallowfield Railway Station was opened. The eight mile long Fallowfield Loop – an off-road cycle path, pedestrian and horse riding route follows the route of the former Fallowfield Loop railway line, which closed in 1988. It connects Chorlton-cum-Hardy in the west with Fairfield in the east, and passes through Whalley Range, Fallowfield, Levenshulme and Gorton. In the early 20th century the university built halls of residence, the earliest being Ashburne Hall in 1910 in a house donated by the Behrens family. Later in the century the Manchester Corporation tramway on Moseley and Wilbraham Roads led the way swiftly into Manchester city centre and back.

As the housing of central Manchester got progressively slummier, insanitary and fetid, the prosperous middle classes built their posh houses here in the 1850s: these included Egerton Lodge, Norton House and Oak House, and the Manchester architect Alfred Waterhouse of Manchester Town Hall fame built Barcombe Cottage for himself on Oak Drive.

The 'Toast Rack', once known as the Hollings Building or College, is a Modernist building completed in 1960 as the Domestic Trades College. On 1st January 1977 Hollings and Didsbury College of Education were amalgamated with Manchester Polytechnic, later to become the Metropolitan University until closure of the "Hollings Campus" in 2013. Its striking architecture reflects its origins as a catering college. Nikolaus Pevsner described the building as "a perfect piece of pop architecture". English Heritage described the Grade II listed structure as, "a distinctive and memorable building which

demonstrates this architect's [Leonard Cecil Howitt] love of structural gymnastics in a dramatic way". To others the building encapsulates the spirit of the 1951 Festival of Britain. It is highly practical: the tapering shape provides different sized teaching spaces for small or large classes, the tailoring workshops were kept separate to minimise noise from the sewing machines, and "The Fried Egg" – comprised a circular hall intended for catwalk shows, the library and two refectories.

Ashburne Hall, and its annexe Sheavyn House, is a University of Manchester hall of residence on the Fallowfield Campus. It was founded in 1900 by Samuel Alexander, R. D. Darbishire, C. P. Scott and Alice B. Cooke as a hall of residence for women students and was first located at Ashburne House in Victoria Park until it moved to "The Oaks" which was then renamed Ashburne Hall in 1910. The new site is on Wilmslow Road at the corner of Old Hall Lane, Fallowfield. The hall had been extended with new buildings by 1930 and benefited from Lord Morley's bequest of his personal library. Sheavyn House was later built in the grounds and commemorates Dr. Sheavyn, a one-time warden of the hall.

Convent of F.C.J. Fallowfield, South View.

The Hollies Convent FCJ School was a girls' direct-grant Roman Catholic grammar school. Which opened at the Hollies in 1900, seventy years after Marie-Madeleine d'Houët (1781–1858), also known as Marie Madeleine Victoire, founded the society of the Faithful Companions of Jesus in Amiens, France. The University of Manchester acquired the site in the late 1950s for student accommodation as part of the Fallowfield Campus; the school decamped to a new site at West Didsbury in 1961; a new prep school was built at the same time.

Domestic Science at the Hollies Convent FCJ School in Mersey Road in the 1970s. 520 girls joined the new £250,000 school in Didsbury in grounds of sixteen acres. By 1973 the number of girls had risen to around 720. Actresses Caroline Aherne and Paula Wilcox are old girls of the school. The Hollies High School closed in 1985.

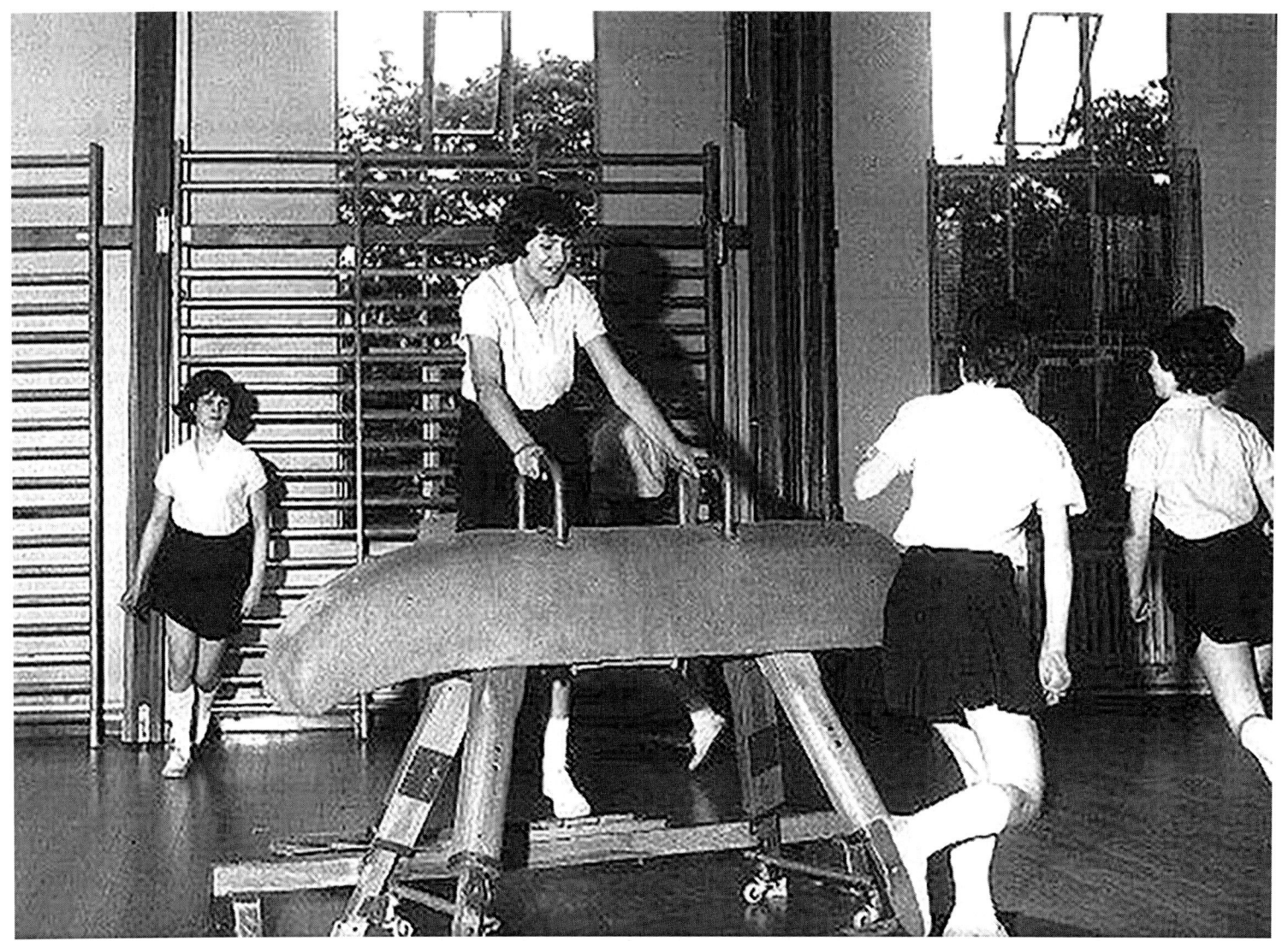

P.T. at the Hollies in the 1970s.

During the 1960s and 1970s, the annual football match, which had started at Fallowfield, continued on its own playing fields. The Hollies enjoyed a relationship with Manchester United Football Club through its manager Matt Busby. Each year Matt and some players went to the school to referee and act as linesmen. The photo shows Sir Matt Busby and George Best at a school event. The event was a mini FA Cup Final with the "little boys" taking centre stage, accompanied by a piper and other rituals associated with a cup final. When George Best refereed the match, the FCJs were 'stretched to the limit of their control, particularly of the teenage members of the school. Keeping high standards was always difficult and it was necessary not to lower the aims of the school.'

This beautiful mansion, Grangethorpe, on the southern edge of Platt Fields was built in the early 1880s in eleven acres for the Moseley family, Manchester industrialists in the manufacture of rubber products. After the Moseley family departed Grangethorpe eventually became the home of Herbert Smith-Carrington, a director of the Whitworth-Armstrong engineering company. On his death in March 1917 the mansion was purchased by the East Lancashire branch of the Red Cross Society with a view to creating a home for disabled war casualties; it was registered under the name 'East Lancs Home for Disabled Sailors and Soldiers'. However, the acute shortage of orthopaedic beds triggered a change in purpose so, from the outset, Grangethorpe was established as an orthopaedic hospital with six wards, an operating block, gymnasium, nurses' home, out-patient clinic and rehabilitation workshops in the gardens. The orthopaedic department at Ducie Avenue School relocated to Grangethorpe.

In 1919 Grangethorpe Hospital was taken over by the Ministry of Pensions, which was responsible for injured war veterans. Medical and surgical work on peripheral nerves was pioneered here and it won a reputation for cutting edge work on the reconstruction of damaged limb nerves, tendon transplants and bone grafts. Amongst the staff were eminent surgeons such as Professor Sir Harry Platt. Workshops were converted into a Cripples Training Centre and a new physiotherapy department and x-ray unit were also built. The hospital closed in 1929 and the remaining patients were transferred to the Ministry of Pensions Hospitals at Liverpool and Leeds. The property was given to Manchester Royal Infirmary but it was too costly to maintain so was sold in 1936 to Manchester High School for Girls. Most of the old Grangethorpe buildings were destroyed through rebuilding and as the photo shows by a German landmine in December 1940 some three months after the girls had moved in. The school was rebuilt and reopened in 1951.

This is a 1917 photo of the 155 bed Moseley Road School in use as a Military Hospital for 'Other Ranks'. Nearby over 1200 beds were provided under canvas in the grounds of The Firs, off Oak Drive, Fallowfield. Fairview, on Wilbraham Road, was acquired by the Red Cross and used as a hospital initially with 20 beds soon rising to 36 beds.

South Manchester Synagogue, seen here in 1911, was founded in 1872 to cater for Ashkenazi families who lived in the south of the city. In 1913 the community moved from Sidney Street, Chorlton on Medlock, to a new building in Wilbraham Road, Fallowfield – its home for nearly 90 years. The listed building results from a competition won by Joseph Sunlight who adopted the style of a Turkish mosque, complete with dome and minaret; Sunlight confessed to being influenced by Hagia Sophia in Istanbul and the tower of London's Westminster Cathedral. The synagogue flourished for many years, due largely to successive waves of refugees from Europe in the 1930s. An extension had to be built to the women's gallery to cater for this. Membership was at over 800 during the 1970s. In 2002, the community relocated to new premises in Bowdon.

Fallowfield Stadium was an athletics stadium and velodrome which opened in 1892 as the home of Manchester Athletics Club which had to move from its home next to Old Trafford Cricket Ground. Fallowfield was most often used for cycling by the Manchester Wheelers' Club, who held their annual competition there until 1976.

The 1893 FA Cup final between Wolverhampton Wanderers and Everton was the stadium's finest hour. Wolves won 1–0, the goal scored by Harry Allen. The stadium had a capacity of 15,000 so when 45,000 spectators got in, very few of them could see the match. Play was impeded so much by encroachment that Everton unsuccessfully demanded a replay afterwards, arguing that the stadium was not fit for purpose. The stadium also hosted the second 1899 FA Cup semi-final replay between Sheffield United and Liverpool; this match had to be abandoned due to a crush in the crowd.

In the early 1960s Manchester University bought Fallowfield Stadium. It was demolished in 1994; the site is now the Richmond Park Halls of Residence, part of the Fallowfield Campus.

Fallowfield Railway Station was on Wilmslow Road on the Fallowfield Loop railway line, a suburban railway which looped around the south of the city and terminated at the former Manchester Central Railway Station. The Manchester, Sheffield and Lincolnshire Railway opened the first section of the Fallowfield Loop line between Chorlton-cum-Hardy and Fallowfield in 1891. The following year saw the remaining section between Fallowfield and Fairfield open. The station closed to passengers in 1958, but its building, on the corner of Wilmslow Road and Ladybarn Road, still stands as part of a supermarket. After its closure to passenger traffic the line was used by freight trains until it closed completely in 1988, with the station's sidings being used by the London Brick Company. The track bed has been repurposed as a cycle path from Gorton to Chorlton. The section of line from Old Trafford to Manchester Central has been re-opened as part of the Manchester Metrolink tram system.

Wilmslow Road with the station on the right. This major artery runs from Parrs Wood northwards to Rusholme where it becomes Oxford Road and the name changes again to Oxford Street when it crosses the River Medlock and reaches the city centre. On the way it takes in major areas of student accommodation, the wonderful curry mile, the Manchester Royal Infirmary and the two Manchester universities and medical school. Wilmslow Road, Oxford Road and Oxford Street form part of an 18th-century route from Manchester to Oxford, and then on to Southampton. The route goes via Cheadle, Cheadle Hulme, Wilmslow, Congleton, Newcastle-under-Lyme, Stafford, Birmingham, Stratford-upon-Avon and Woodstock.

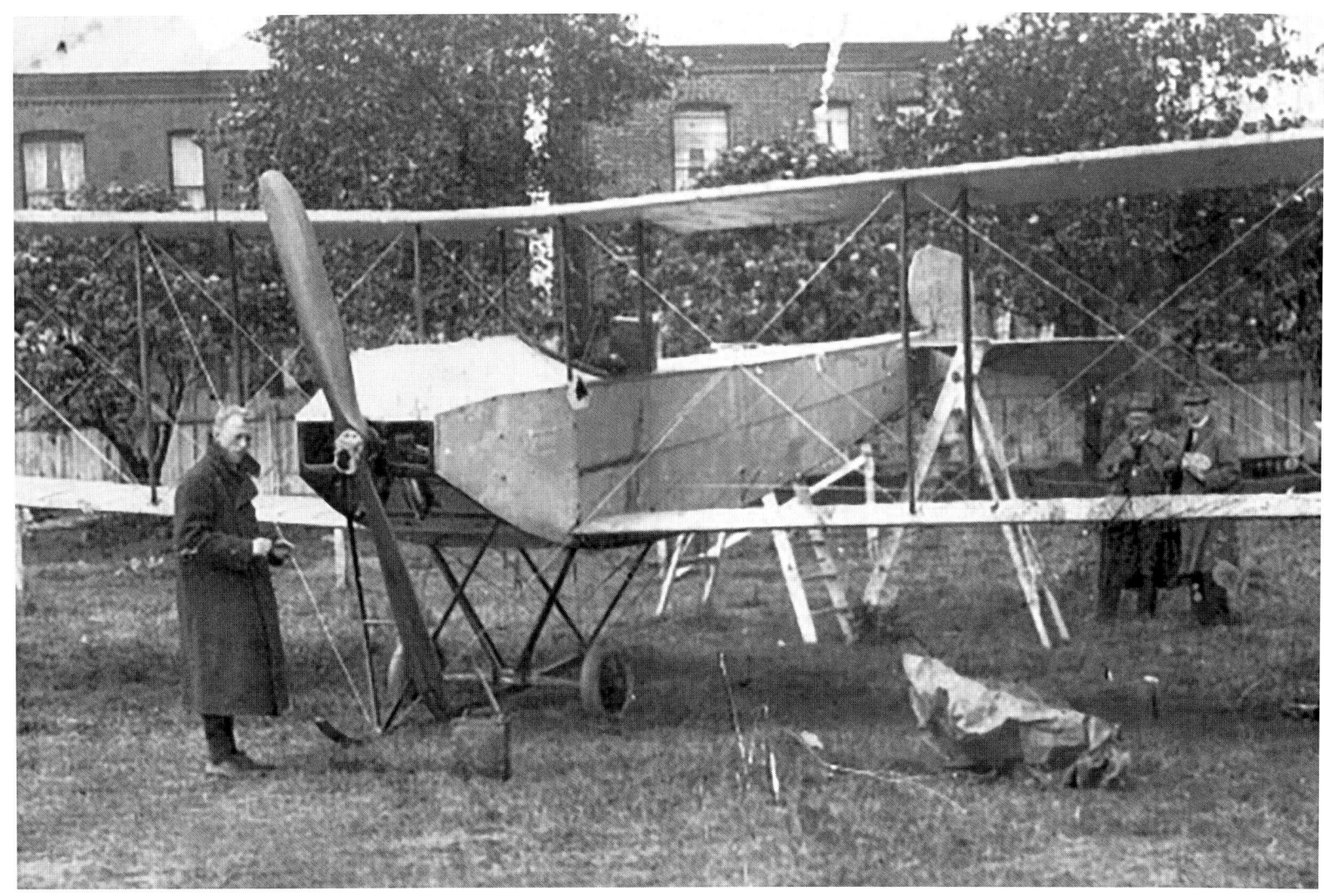

The first flight into Fallowfield landed in 1912; the pilot was a Mr. Yoxall who flew the Avro 500 biplane from Trafford Park Aerodrome into a temporary airstrip here.

Photographer: Ringwayobserver.

After the closure of Trafford Park Aerodrome, Alexandra Park Aerodrome, three miles south of Manchester's city centre, was built and opened in May 1918 by the War Department for the assembly, test flying and delivery to the RAF of aeroplanes built by A. V. Roe & Company (Avro) at Newton Heath and the National Aircraft Factory No. 2 (NAF No.2) at Heaton Chapel. Many aeroplanes were brought by rail from them to the station near the aerodrome. The Avro Transport Company operated the UK's first scheduled domestic air service from Alexandra Park via Birkdale Sands (Southport) to South Shore (Blackpool) between 24th May and 30th September 1919, mainly using Avro 504 three-seat biplanes. From 1922 until 1924 Daimler Airways operated daily scheduled passenger flights to Croydon Airport, later followed by a regular extension to Schiphol Airport, Amsterdam. Because air travel was seen as being very dangerous, the ticket agent, Messrs. Robinsons of Whalley Range, developed a system to reassure travellers relatives. Upon a safe landing at Croydon Airport, a telegram was despatched to Robinsons' office, on receipt of which a messenger boy was despatched in turn to the travellers' homes to report the good news. On the evening of 14th September 1923 the northbound de Havilland DH.34 ten-seat biplane airliner crashed near Ivinghoe Beacon in the Chilterns during an attempted forced landing in bad weather. The two pilots and three passengers were killed, making this the first fatal accident on an internal air service in the UK: the route was suspended for a period. The aerodrome closed to air traffic on 24th August 1924, and the hangars were demolished.

24033 Platt Hall, Platt Fields, Manchester.

Platt Hall was the home of the Worsley family for 300 years. The current hall, a listed Georgian building, was built by John and Deborah Carill-Worsley to the designs of John Carr of York, later modified by Timothy Lightoler, in 1746 at a cost of £10,000. It replaced a timbered black and white building that had been the home of Charles Worsley, one of Cromwell's lieutenants and Major General for Lancashire, Cheshire and Derbyshire during the interregnum. On Cromwell's bidding Charles took away 'that bauble' – meaning the Mace – from the House of Commons and kept it safe until the next sitting of Parliament. Platt Hall contains 'The Gallery of Costume', a 20,000 piece collection owned and operated by Manchester Art Gallery, spanning the 17th century to the present day; it covers clothing worn by men, women and children, and includes both high fashion and the dress of working people.

Platt Abbey on Wilmslow Road was built in the early 19th century but despite the name there was nothing religious about it. It eventually became a hotel and was demolished in 1950. The site was earmarked to be the base for the BBC Northern Studios but Manchester City Council built the two blocks of flats that are still on the site instead. Note the croquet lawn and the beautiful Gothic windows which may account for its ecclesiastical name. Platt Abbey was the home and birthplace of John Hay Beith (1876–1952), the writer whose pen name was Ian Hay, famous for this line from his play, Housemaster: "What do you mean, funny? Funny-peculiar or funny ha-ha?".

Platt Chapel on Wilmslow Road dates from 1791 and was almost totally rebuilt in 1874-76. It was a family chapel of the Worsleys of Platt Hall, itself built in 1699. The congregation was initially Independents (Congregationalists) and became Unitarian during the early 19th century.

The first record of the Platt Estate comes in 1150, when 'Matthew, Son of William' conveyed the "lands of Platt" to the Knights of St. John. In 1225 the estate was acquired by the Platt family who then occupied the lands for the next 400 years until it was taken over by the Worsley family in 1625. At this time, the Platt Hall Estate was a country park on the borders of the Cheshire Plain. In 1907 a resolution was passed recommending the Corporation buy Platt Fields site for public use and thereby save the park and house for future generations; this led to the purchase of the land from Mrs. Elizabeth Tindal-Carill-Worsley, the last owner of the estate, for £59,975 in 1908. During the winter of 1908-09 over 700 unemployed men were given work on laying out the park, inverting the Gore Brook and planting banks with trees and shrubs. The main feature and centrepiece was the construction of a lake and island that covers just over 6 acres. Platt Fields Park was formally opened by the Lord Mayor of Manchester, Councillor Behrens, on 7th May 1910. Between 1919 and 1925 when unemployment was again high, the parks committee provided more work for local people, levelling the park and playing fields, forming the bowling greens, tennis courts and bathing pool. The part of the playing fields overlooked by Trinity Church was once a speaker's corner.

Access to the island was only ever possible by boat. The Main Lake had a large boat house and wood-covered slipway. It housed not only a fleet of large, clinker built rowing boats and skiffs but also a motor launch, the *Archie Littlemore*, which gave rides during the summer months – 'Twice Around the Island'. *The Manchester Guardian* reported that on Saturday 18th July 1914, deprived children from the poorest parts of Manchester had a day out in the park.

The south end of the park, known today as Ashfield, was the grounds of another stately home, built around 1835 and owned by Mr. Robinson 'a well-known Manchester merchant' who had 'extensive pleasure grounds contain(ing) plantations, fishponds and every kind of garden' which included the Shakespearean Garden and the Cathedral Arch which are now in Platt Fields Park. The 15th century Cathedral Arch was a window from Manchester Cathedral, acquired as a folly by Mr. Robinson and placed here near the Nico Ditch in the 19th century when the cathedral nave was being replaced.

Manchester High School for Girls was founded in 1874 by nine prominent men and women of Manchester: it was originally established in Chorlton-on-Medlock; in 1881 a new school was built in Dover Street, now occupied by the University of Manchester School of Social Sciences. In this 1905 photo Miss Caroline Coignou is showing girls a toad.

Girls and teachers in 1899. At the outbreak of war in September 1939 the school was evacuated to Cheadle Hulme; by 1940 a new school building was being built at Fallowfield at the Grangethorpe Road site. The unfinished buildings were destroyed by bombing on 20th December 1940. In 1941 the school moved temporarily to Didsbury and by 1949 a new building at Grangethorpe Road was occupied. The move to the new school was complete by 1952.

Dressmaking in the 1900s. Alumnae include Clara Freeman, the first woman to be appointed to the board of Marks & Spencer; Merlyn Lowther, the first female Chief Cashier of the Bank of England (1999–2004); Libby Lane, the Church of England's first female bishop; Edith Hesling, the first woman barrister called to the bar at Gray's Inn; Catherine Chisholm (1879–1952), Manchester High School doctor: 1908–44, GP and paediatrician, and the first woman to graduate from Manchester University Medical School in 1904. She was also founder of the Manchester Babies Hospital (later the Duchess of York Hospital) in 1914. In 1950 she became the first woman to be awarded an honorary Fellowship by the Royal College of Physicians; Eileen Derbyshire, played Emily Bishop in *Coronation Street*; and Julia Bodmer, née Pilkington, Manchester High School pupil: 1945–53, discovered the details of the human leukocyte antigen (HLA) with genetic differences causing transplant rejection.

Manchester High for Girls and staff had a very busy First World War. They worked in local Red Cross hospitals as nurses and ancillary staff, acted as interpreters for Belgian soldiers who were patients in Manchester hospitals and made prodigious amounts of jam and clothes for patients. One old girl worked as a doctor in Serbia, another member of staff worked with the Quakers in France but died of typhoid. Some scholarships were endowed for the daughters of sailors, one of the school magazines contains a letter from the officer on a torpedo boat destroyer who signed himself "Chevalier of the Legion of Sea Hun Strafers".

Senior girls in a 1900s secretarial class with Miss Kiero Moore, standing on the right. The school's association with the Pankhursts is particularly strong: Adela Pankhurst, Manchester High School pupil, 1893–1902, campaigner in the Australian suffragette movement; Christabel Pankhurst, 1893–97, the first woman to be awarded an LLB degree by Manchester University, founder member of the Women's Social and Political Union and leading campaigner in the British suffragette movement – sister of Sylvia Pankhurst, 1893–98.

Manchester Grammar School is the largest UK independent day school for boys; founded in 1515 as a free grammar school – the Manchester Free Grammar School for Lancashire Boys – next to Manchester Cathedral (Manchester's Parish Church).

By 1808 there were efforts to relocate the school; Engels, in his *The Condition of the Working Class in England*, said of the insalubrious area: 'Going from the Old Church to Long Millgate ... one is in an almost undisguised working men's quarter, for even the shops and beerhouses hardly take the trouble to exhibit a trifling degree of cleanliness ... [The Irk, next to the school] is a narrow, coal black, foul smelling stream full of debris and refuse.'

Long Millgate was the main route to reach the Collegiate Church from the north side of the town but even by 1817 it was seen as a dead end, physically and metaphorically. Procter, writing in his *Memorials of Manchester Streets,* said "For most useful and ornamental purposes, this street, ruthlessly cut into many pieces, has been virtually dead for many years, only requiring to be put decently out of sight".

Richard Wright Procter (1816–1881) was an English barber, poet and author. The son of poor parents he was born in Paradise Vale, Salford. Apprenticed to a barber, he set up in business for himself in Long Millgate, where he also ran a circulating library. He remained there for the rest of his life.

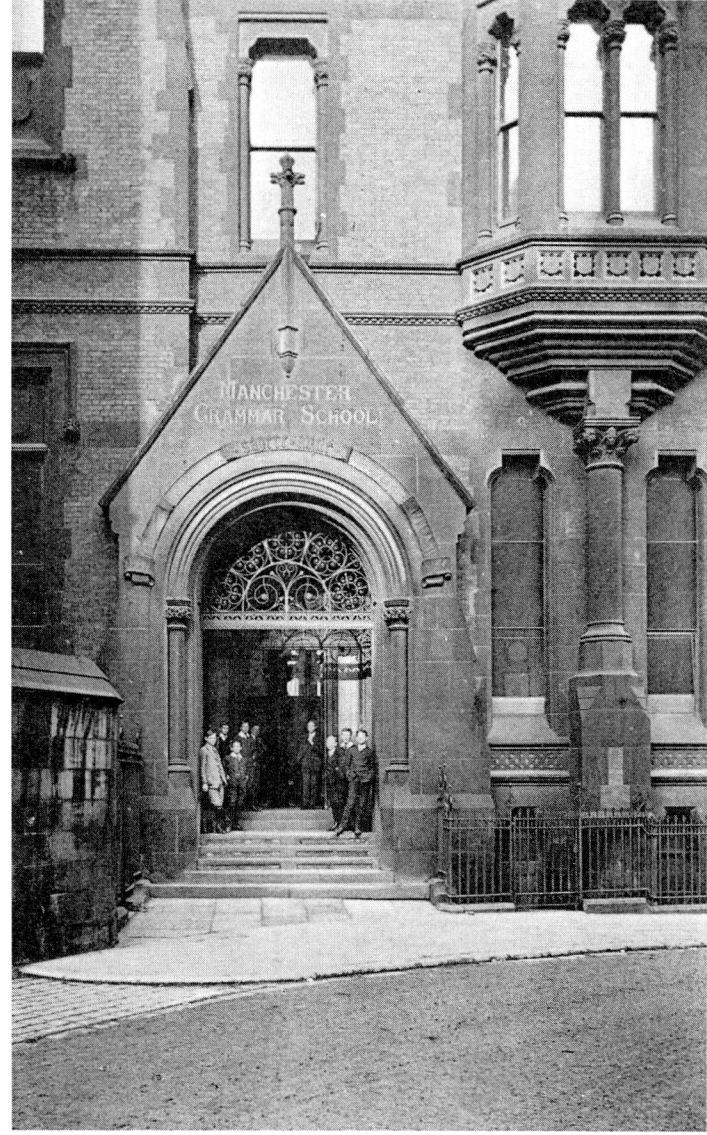

In 1931 the school moved to its present site at Fallowfield and the photo shows it on the first day. The original deed promoted "Godliness and good learning" and established that any boy showing sufficient academic ability, regardless of background, might attend, free of charge. It was remarkably enlightened and provided a school house in the curtilage of Manchester's Parish Church and two graduates (the 'High Master' and the 'Usher') to teach Latin and later Greek, to any children who presented themselves. The school was intended to prepare pupils for university and eventually the Church or the legal profession. There was usually enough money available to fund bursaries or exhibitions for pupils.

The Michael Atherton Sports Hall was opened by old boy Mike Atherton in 1997. A new sports hall opened in 2016. By the 18th century, there were between 50 and 100 boys in the grammar school, three or four of whom each year were awarded exhibitions to Oxford and Cambridge. An extra room was built onto the school house for boys who needed coaching in English before they started Latin, and a master was employed to teach them.

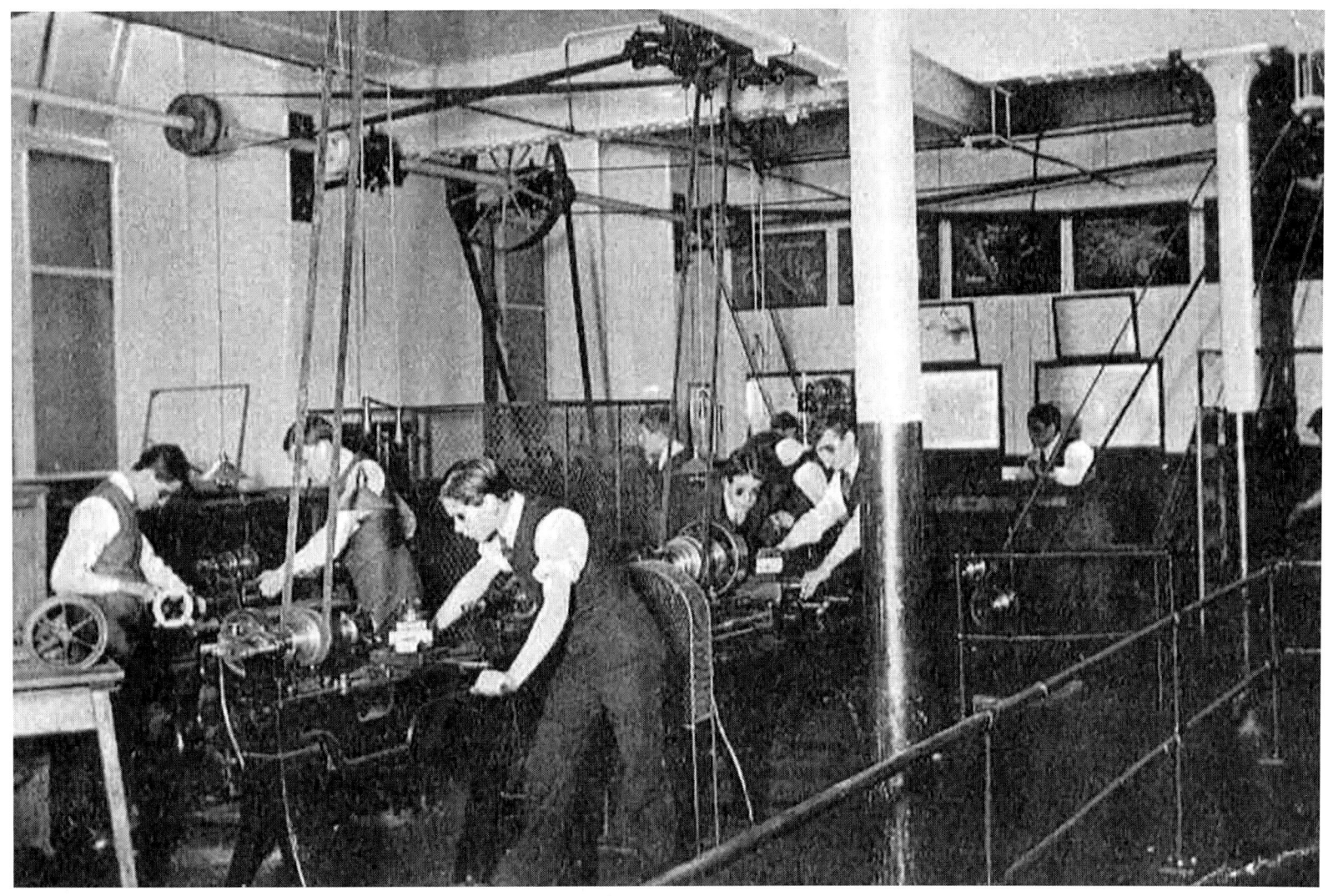

Long Millgate workshop. Note the eye protection. Many of the Upper School for the Latin and Greek pupils were boarders from surrounding counties. When Thomas De Quincy came as a boarder in 1800, classes were at 7.00am to 9.00, 9.30 to 12.00 and 3.00pm to 5.00.

Long Millgate biology classroom. Stuffed birds and animals at the back. The Sieff Theatre is named after Israel Moses Sieff (chairman of Marks & Spencer from 1964 to 1967) and is used for lectures and assemblies, as well as being the venue to Muslim Friday prayers.

Free school milk started with the 1906 Education (Provision of Meals) Act, which allowed Local Education Authorities to deliver free school meals, including milk. Surprisingly, not all LEAs availed themselves of this even though milk had long been recognised as helping undernourished children – good nutrition having been identified as key to effective learning; by the end of the 1930s not even half were offering the free meals. In 1945 Ellen Wilkinson, the Minister of Education under Clement Atlee (the first woman to take the post and anti-poverty champion) was influential in having Parliament pass the Free School Milk Act which gave every school child under 18 the right to a third of a pint of milk each day.

The common room in 1954. The 'master' on the right is having a particularly bad day. This is a rare photograph: staff rooms at this time were usually obscured in a fog of cigarette and pipe smoke making the clarity of this image all the more remarkable.

The school's alumni are called Old Mancs, and include former England cricket captain Mike Atherton, Thomas de Quincey, playwright Robert Bolt, journalist and broadcaster Martin Sixsmith, actors Ben Kingsley and Robert Powell, and historian Michael Wood.

A tuck shop typically sells confectionery, sandwiches, crisps, soft drinks and the like. More often than not we associate them with schools but they can refer to any small, food-selling retailer. The origin of tuck probably comes from the popular shops run by members of the Tuck family between 1780 and 1850. The earliest reference found is to Thomas Tuck whose "Tuck's Coffee House" in Norwich was popular among the city's literary circles in the late 18th century and which had a library for the use of customers.

Sandbagging in the early 1940s. Today the main building houses the Parker Art Hall which is a three storey arts studio and includes a ceramics department with two kilns and a dark room for photography. The MGS Theatre offers a modern auditorium, together with studios for rehearsals and drama teaching.

Mellor's Farm and Grundy's Farm, both in Ladybarn Lane remind us of just how rural Fallowfield was in the early 20th century. Mary Broom's farm is the subject of a watercolour painted in 1874 by William Laithwood Appleton. Other farms were Old Hall Farm, Demesne Farm; Large Oak Farm, Small Oak Farm, Firs Farm and Dog House Farm. Firs Farm went on to be absorbed into the Manchester Athletic Club grounds established on Whitworth Lane in 1891 which included a banked cycle track. In 1955 the grounds were bought by Reg Harris, a famous Manchester racing cyclist, and renamed the Harris Stadium. Manchester University bought the grounds and built the Owens Park Student Village Complex on the site. Manchester Harriers & Athletics Club continues to thrive at Wythenshawe Park. If you're going there it should not be confused with Manchester Athletic Club, located in Manchester-by-the-Sea, Massachusetts.

Mellor's Farm on Ladybarn Road about 1890. Mrs. W.C. Williamson, in her 1888 *Fallowfield: Sketches of Fallowfield and the surrounding Manors, Past & Present* described it: 'On the opposite or Burnage side of Fallowfield are Large Oak, built by the son of Major-General Worsley, and for so long occupied by the same family that we know it only as "Mellor's," and "Little Oak," now occupied by Mr. Grundy, formerly by Farmer Lithgo, the father of Mrs. Mellor. Nearer Birch, and on the same side the high road, is a cosy house, in which long ago the parent Mellor flourished, and from which he sent out children, and children's children, until the whole neighbourhood appeared to be farmed by Mellors.' Ladybarn Road gets its name from the tithe barn that stood here named after Our Lady.

Mauldeth Road probably gets its name from Mauldeth Hall in Heatons North, a large Greek Revival villa, built in 1832-60, for Joseph Chessborough Dyer. It was bought in 1854 as a residence for the Bishops of Manchester and extended in 1880-82 by Charles Heathcote so that it could become a hospital for incurables. After its restoration in the 1990s, the hall became the residence of the Consul General of the People's Republic of China in Manchester. The Talbot Hotel was demolished in 2010; after being a Threlfall's house it was taken over by Whitbread. It was later called the Peninsular and finally the Ladybarn. It was once run by Frank Swift, the Manchester City goalkeeper who died in the Munich Air Disaster in 1958 along with eight United players and fourteen others.

Fallowfield is bisected east-west by Wilmslow Road and north-south by Moseley Road and Wilbraham Road. During the first half of the 20th century the Manchester Corporation tramway on Moseley and Wilbraham Roads gave access to other southern suburbs and to the city centre via Princess Road. The photo shows works extending the tramlines on Moseley Road in 1904: in 1895 Rusholme and the northern part of Fallowfield were incorporated into the city of Manchester; the extension coincided with the whole of the urban district being absorbed into the city of Manchester in 1904.

Braemar Road, Fallowfield

A Manchester Laundry cart delivering and collecting laundry in Braemar Road with a grocer's just in shot on the near right. There was a pub here at nos. 74-76 called the Old House at Home, one of four in Manchester with another in Didsbury-Withington. The Braemar Road backstreet local closed in 2010 and is now student accommodation. The planning document lamented the loss of the pub as "…regrettable as it represented a community facility that facilitated social cohesion" which tells us what a tight knit community the Braemar Road area was. The Old House at Home was hidden away on Braemar Road, parallel to Moseley Road. Today the area is synonymous with student accommodation.

The Red Lion is a 17th century coaching inn on the Wilmslow Road. Grade II listed, is still in business today. The pub was home to a local court, the Withington Court Leet, until 1841, and the meeting place for the Trustees of the Turnpike Trust for what is today Wilmslow Road. The Red Lion used to be at the centre of the "rush cart procession" which took place on St. Oswald's Day, August 5th. The rushes, which Withington provided to strew on the floor of the Parish Church at Didsbury, were heaped high onto a large waggon and escorted with mime and dancing. This procession was held for over 600 years, surviving well into the 19th century. In later years, the rush cart was made up at Mee's Farm, at the back of the 'White Lion'. Sometimes the date 1603 was fashioned in marigolds on the cart. Fletcher Moss suggested that this date indicated when a cart was first used to carry the rushes. Before it, men or pack horses would have been used.